Magic

CRYSTAL
BALL

T0364081

Running Press
Hachette Book Group
1290 Avenue of the Americas, New York, NY 10104
www.runningpress.com
@Running_Press

First Edition: September 2018

Published by Running Press, an imprint of Perseus Books, LLC,
a subsidiary of Hachette Book Group, Inc. The Running Press
name and logo is a trademark of the Hachette Book Group.

The publisher is not responsible for websites (or their content)
that are not owned by the publisher.

ISBN: 978-0-7624-6514-9

CONTENTS

THE ANCIENT ART OF CRYSTAL GAZING

～ceeee~

People have had a connection to crystals and stones throughout the history of mankind. These fascinating minerals date back millions of years to when they first formed on earth, providing plenty of time for humans to discover their uses for protection, healing, and guidance. In spiritual practices, it is still believed by many that crystals and stones have the power to protect us from unwanted negative energies, such as ill-wishes from others, jealousy, and other unkind feelings that come our way. It was believed in many ancient cultures, including Roman, Egyptian, Chinese, Greek, Indian, and Japanese, that they could help in finding emotional and spiritual balance. They have been thought to open the door for energies that get tucked into the mind, body, and spirit, helping them to flow freely, and thus unlocking highly sought after answers and information.

Crystals and stones are in a category of powerful tools that are used for divination practices.

The ancient art of divination is a complex form of fortune telling, which can use many other sources of power to help forecast the future or gain insight. Crystals, in particular, are thought to have the power to reveal images that come from spirits or the unconscious mind. Finding these images of truth have always been desired by humans because they were thought to reveal

important hidden knowledge of the past, present, and future.

Divination and fortune telling can be traced as far back as the ancient Celtic druid civilizations. The druids, who inhabited Gaul, Britain, and Ireland, were a class of educators, judges, and priests who spent most of their time in the forests. Druids were not only the source of all information, but also the primary authority on public and private disagreements. Before the druids were eventually wiped out by Christianity, they were known to implement a variety of methods to obtain information. Nature and weather were important tools that they had at their disposal, and they would observe clouds, trees, and the behavior of animals to divine information.

CRYSTAL BALLS: A MINI HISTORY

ecceee

After the druids vanished, the symbolic icon of the crystal ball began to rise and take shape sometime during the Middle Ages and continued through the Renaissance period. Early crystal gazers would use polished spheres made of the mineral Beryl, a type of gemstone that often has a tint of green, blue, or yellow color. Beryl has a stronger magnetic charge than other gemstones and it was thought to have a better connection to psychic energies. By the 15th century, crystal spheres were seen as a symbol of class and power, and it is believed that Anglo-Saxons would carry

around crystal spheres as both a spiritual talisman and a fashion accessory.

When the Romani people began to migrate from India to Europe starting in the 14th century, the nomadic group brought with them a wealth of trades and services to European culture, including metal work, horse dealing, music, entertainment, and last but not least, the magic of fortune telling. This is most likely how the crystal ball became a prominent icon in fortune telling, which eventually brought about the carnival trope of the traveling, crystal ball gazing, fortune teller. Perhaps you will recall the traveling gypsy, Professor Marvel, in *The Wizard of Oz*, of whom Dorothy pays a visit?

As fortune telling grew in popularity as a form of entertainment, particularly in traveling magic acts of the 20th century, so did the crystal ball. Popular culture also played a role in generating the many mischaracterizations and stereotypes of fortune tellers, and one of the most popular was the scarf-wearing gypsy holding a powerful looking crystal ball.

This character was used in fortune telling machines and, at the time, only cost a dime to receive a fortune. Many of these machines were and can still be found at carnivals and arcades, and the mischaracterization of the Roma fortune teller is, surprisingly, still familiar even today.

What has unfortunately become lost in the narrow

stereotypes of fortune telling is the larger path on which crystal ball gazing can take us. The empowering nature of the crystal ball goes beyond the simple gesture of looking into a ball to see into the future. If we open ourselves up to it, crystal gazing can help amplify our feelings that are hidden in the mind, therefore providing us with insight that may have otherwise gone untapped. To better understand this, let us now explore the last ritual of crystal ball gazing.

SCRYING: WHAT IS IT AND HOW TO DO IT

The act of looking into a particular object in order to perceive mystical information is referred to as scrying. Scrying involves a ritual of putting oneself in a meditative trance, allowing the scryer to access the unconscious mind for unlocking information of the past, present, and future. Scrying can also be done with many forms of fortune telling, such as reading tarot cards, palm reading, and interpreting tea leaves or coffee grounds. Although more uncommon, back in the earlier days of divination, people were

also known to scry with other types of reflective surfaces such as mirrors, glass, water, and even blood.

When it comes to crystal ball gazing, scrying is not as simple as staring into the reflective surface and seeing the answer right in front of you. The art of scrying requires deep relaxation and mental concentration. In order to become better at scrying, practicing meditation can be very beneficial. Focusing on clearing your mind of any distractions is key in order to get the most out of scrying. In the next section, we will provide some helpful tips on how practice scrying with your crystal ball.

TIPS FOR USING YOUR CRYSTAL BALL

~ perese ~

Divination and fortune telling isn't just for the experts. You, too, can unlock the knowledge you are seeking if you open up your mind and allow it to go, where it needs to go.

It is important to remember that the crystal ball is only a tool. Your mind is what will be doing most of the work when you practice crystal ball gazing. Although the crystal ball in this kit may seem to provide you with decisive answers to your questions, the answers you hear will be open-ended and helpful for deeper understanding. The answers can be thought of as a first step to unlocking more detailed information that you can explore with your crystal ball further. In other words, don't be afraid to go beyond what the crystal ball tells you. You might just be able to uncover more than you expected.

In order to begin accessing your unconscious, be sure to

place yourself in a quiet area of your home or office that is not easily disrupted. Practicing in the dark with lit candles can be a nice calming atmosphere for getting yourself in the ball gazing mood. Some gazers also prefer burning incense and playing tranquil music to help clear the mind.

After you have cultivated and settled into your calming space,

begin to relax by inhaling and exhaling deeply for several minutes so that your breath becomes steady and rhythmic. Close your eyes and allow yourself to clear the mind of any distractions. What is your mind wandering to? Focusing on wherever your mind takes you is the best place to begin reflecting on a question, idea, or challenge that occurs in your thoughts. When you feel your question coming to life, then you will know what to ask the crystal ball.

If you are having trouble seeing a question forming in your mind, fear not. Patience is key. Some questions you can ask include: Will I find love? Am I making good decisions? Will I find my special talents?

If you hear positive answers from your crystal ball, such as "It is certain" or "Without a doubt," do not stop there. Keep your mind open to other feedback that could be flowing with information from within. Look out for any images that form in your head as you peer deeper into your crystal ball. Perhaps they will lead you closer the truth, or to something else entirely unexpected.

If you receive replies that are indecisive, such as "Reply hazy, try again" or "Concentrate and try again," this may mean that you need to spend more time meditating on your question. Once your question becomes clearer, ask your crystal ball again what you are

trying to look for. Remember, continual practice will help with understanding the delicate art of crystal-ball gazing. Before you become too frustrated, take a break from the crystal ball, and return to it when you are feeling more energized.

Finally, you may be disappointed to hear answers from the ball that you were not hoping for.

Again, do not be discouraged. Discovering unwanted information is simply a part of the scrying process. If you continue meditating, you may be able to unlock more pieces of the mystifying puzzle that could prove useful in future day-to-day experiences. What you discover now may be helpful at another point in time or when you least expect it.

ANSWERS
FROM YOUR
CRYSTAL BALL

※ ⁕⁕⁕⁕⁕

Here is the full list of answers that your crystal ball will reveal out loud. However, these answers don't stop here. You can use these open-ended answers as a starting point in your crystal ball gazing journey. Remember, you and you alone are the one who holds the true answers to your future!

IT IS CERTAIN.

WITHOUT A DOUBT.

YES, DEFINITELY.

MOST LIKELY.

OUTLOOK GOOD.

REPLY HAZY, TRY AGAIN.

ASK AGAIN LATER.

BETTER NOT TELL YOU NOW.

CANNOT PREDICT NOW.

CONCENTRATE AND
ASK AGAIN.

DON'T COUNT ON IT.

MY REPLY IS NO.

MY SOURCES SAY NO.

OUTLOOK NOT
SO GOOD.

VERY DOUBTFUL.

This book has been bound
using handcraft methods and
Smyth-sewn to ensure
durability.

Written by Marlo Scrimizzi.

Designed and illustrated
by Jason Kayser.